The Book of Knots and Their Untying

The Book of Knots and Their Untying

Poems by

Karen Greenbaum-Maya

Karen Greenbaum-Maya (signature)

Kelsay Books

© 2016 Karen Greenbaum-Maya. All rights reserved. This material may not be reproduced in any form, published, reprinted, recorded, performed, broadcast, rewritten or redistributed without the explicit permission of Karen Greenbaum-Maya. All such actions are strictly prohibited by law.

Cover: Karen Greenbaum-Maya

ISBN 13: 978-1-945752-18-6

Kelsay Books
Aldrich Press
www.kelsaybooks.com

Acknowledgments

The notes on knots that appear on the section divider pages are adapted from Wikipedia's entries on the specific types of knots.

The left-hand text of "Opioid Withdrawal/Total Eclipse" is taken passim from the Wikipedia entry on opioid withdrawal. The right-hand text is my own free translation of Adelbert Stifter's account of 1837.

I wish to thank the following publications where some of these poems appeared previously in similar versions.

Black Lawrence Press Anthology, FEAST: "Eggs Satori"
Blue Lyra Review: "My Uncle the Perfectionist"
B O D Y: "carpet, n. v.," "Bob Hope at the River Glen Psych Unit"
The Centrifugal Eye: "Dayenu/Genug," "Glow-worm," "I Will Not Die in Cochabamba," "Older Woman," "Opioid Withdrawal/Total Eclipse," "Perspective," "Stop and try our homemade pie"
Comstock Poetry Review: "Real Poem," Honorable Mention, 2013 Muriel Comstock Bailey Poetry Contest. "Knots and Their Untying," Special Merit, 2016 Muriel Comstock Bailey Poetry contest.
Conclave, a journal of character: "Our Lady of the Red Potatoes" Pushcart nominee 2015
Dirty Napkin: "Pear"
dotdotdash: "Eggs Satori"
Flutter Poetry Review: "Ghazal of Wasted Time"
The Furnace Review: "Double Abecedarian at Forest Lawn"
Good Works Anthologies, Aging: "Dignitas"
Heron Tree: "Ariel echo of Prospero"
Inlandia: "Hard-Boiled Egg," "Throwbacks"
Kattywompus Press, Burrowing Song: "Bob Hope at the River Glen Psych Unit," "Burrowing Song," "Papa"
Kind of a Hurricane Press, Tic Toc: "Ghazal before Memory,"

"Silence and Slow Time"
Lilliput Review: "Older Woman"
Mobius: a journal of social change: "Passing Through"
Mom Egg: "Acknowledgments, In Other Words"
Off the Coast: "Oneiric CV" ,"Papa"
One Sentence Poetry: "Oak Apples"
Perfume River Review: "Monsieur Saluki"
Poemeleom: "So Sorry"
Psychic Meatloaf: "'Still Life with Anemones','Room at Arles'"
qarrtsiluni: "The Babinski," "Burrowing Song"
quickly: "fat, adj., n."
Right Hand Pointing: "Body of Knots," "Two-Wheeler"
Riverbabble: "Aha: Atomic Apron"
RiverLit: "Macht Frei","Northern Lights"
San Gabriel Valley Poetry Quarterly: "Less Passionate Ghazal"
Sow's Ear Poetry Review: "Dayenu/Genug," "Dignitas"
TrainWrite/tumblr: "Conductor"
Unshod Quills: "Donut Slam"
Women's Studies Quarterly: "Twiggy and Me"

Contents

Body of Knots
SQUARE

Glow-Worm	15
fat, adj.,n.	16
Donut Slam	17
Eggs Satori	19
Hard-Boiled Egg	21
Dignitas	22
Pear	23
Opioid Withdrawal/Total Eclipse	24
carpet, n., v.	25
Ghazal of Wasted Time	26
Throwbacks	27
Beautiful Leaves	28

SLIP

Aha: Atomic Apron	33
So Sorry	34
Silence and Slow Time	36
Less Passionate Ghazal	37
Ariel echo of Prospero	38
Twiggy and Me	39
Two-Wheeler	41
Metaphor Blew Them Away	42
Perspective	43
Endless Water	44
Disco Jukebox Sestina Blues	45
Oak Apples	47
The Blues	48

GRANNY

Acknowledgement, In Other Words	51
Papa	52
Bel Canto for the King	53
History, with Rugelach	54
My Mother the Illusionist	55
Bob Hope at the River Glen Psych Unit	56
Jitterbug	57
The Art of Coin Fishing	59
Our Lady of the Red Potatoes	60
To Die in Cochabamba (I Will Not Die in Paris)	61
Fairest	62
Monsieur Saluki	64
Stop and try our Homemade Pie	65
Real Poem	66
Older woman	67
The Babinski	68
Estate Sale	69

GORDIAN

Double Abecedarian at Forest Lawn	73
Conductor	74
Burrowing Song	75
Komisch	76
Passing Through	77
Macht Frei	79
Oneiric CV	80
Northern Lights	81
Planet Janet	82
My Uncle the Perfectionist	83
Ghazal before Memory	84
"Still Life with Anemones," "Room at Arles"	85
Dayenu: Genug	86
Knots and Their Untying	89

About the Author

Body of Knots

Knot, a hard word to write, the small K silent but demanding, needing four strokes, three changes of direction, down-up, out-in, down-and-out. Knots, bumps of wood where the branches leave the trunk and the saw bounces off, every stroke's intention deflected and sent away. See how knots make a body: Turk's Head has a Hole-in-the-Head, the Eye Splice. Throat Knots clutched between Cat's Paw and Monkey's Paw. Underhand Shank balances Underwriter's Shank. Sheep Shank ends in a Lark's Foot.

Knots in knuckles, built by arthritis. Knot-muscled body builder whose arms can't hang down, too strong to move. Knots in my shoulders, muscles pulled tight enraging the places where separate muscles meet, the angry binding of two, too much asked too often. Knots in curly hair, forced by brute-forcing the brush from the root on out. Why not start at the ends where the load is small? Why pull so hard that every knot turns Gordian? Knot in my stomach, working to digest the thing that is no thing, indigestible. Keep trying to solve it, dissolve it before it eats a hole, a hole that can't be knotted shut.

Hear the power of knots, handed down in names: Widow-Maker, God-Forsaker, Meet-Your-Maker, Phantom-Staker, Slip Square Reef, and Thief, and Granny.

SQUARE

—also known as Reef Knot, Hercules Knot, Surgeon's Knot. Origin is ancient.

Glow-Worm

See my mother in labor, cursing me out.
Six blocks up Sunset Boulevard
in the Capitol basement studio
under LP stories layered up like cake,
Billie Holiday is holding nothing back,
finishes up some "Nice Work,"
eyes shut, damp face shining.
And if you get it, won't you tell me how?
Lady Day says, "I've got one more in me,"
and her combo floats into "Blue Moon".
That same night, a flotilla of UFOs passes
over Hollywood Presbyterian Hospital.
Shine little glow-worm, glimmer, glimmer.
Sunset Boulevard's pulsed lights draw them east
to Eva Perón in her hospital room in London.
Her head falls back, last breath floats out.
Mother hears the baby's cry.
Shine little glow-worm, glimmer, glimmer.

fat, adj.,n.

    from Old Middle Frisian
Early Old Norwegian
springing, welling, full
as wine skins stretched to bursting.
Same Greek root as *weight*:
pīd, poid, also pîdax, *gushing forth*;
deeper still, back to Sanskrit:
memory, the way tree rings reveal
seasons of warmth and rain,
of brown rice and kale, umami,
body-records of meatloaf and brownies,
ballet   bicycling   boxing
three, four times a week,
Baryshnikov's torqued knee.
Fat, cinched cells resisting insulin,
a hundred days of *no*
undone by a weekend of *more*.
Fat, holding eons, ice releasing vapor
of not-quite-human life, polar bears
swimming themselves thin thin thin.

Donut Slam

   I admit: I'll wear it if it fits
and I've worn out the F-word,
the only F-word left: F-A-T.
When you see me, it's all you see,
the only thing going in my obit.
I am the elephant in this room.

   Should I prove I'm fit to take up space?
I'm officially unfit, too big to be seen
by long-waisted odalisques, the ones who sit at ease
knowing they'll be asked to dance,
not stranded at the edges wondering what it's like
to be wanted, to be welcomed,
not to be a misfit, not to have to outwit
to be partnered at the party
going on in the world. Do I have to throw a fit?

   Just admit: it's meet and proper, a good close fit
to diet in this rich land,
or you don't fit in, not into the mold,
not into the True Religions.
Just admit: fittest survivors
don't know what they're fit for.
A surfeit of women sit huddled in the sauna,
talking kitchen porn about rich foods forbidden.
Grown women in a snit,
cinched in knots, throwing fits
if their number waxes bigger.
I admit, if folks don't see me, I don't exist.
It's a hit hurts like a fist.

    Even in a battle of wits,
when they say *fat* it's over. You are lost.
Fat's the only mortal sin left to commit.
Can't decrypt my story? Hit this:
I am not finished, and honey,
I am far from done.

Eggs Satori

Take an egg for each eater,
another for the pan.
The eggshells should be opaque,
too bright to look at if white, freckled matte if brown.
Crack the eggs into a generous bowl.
Use your entire arm, wrist hand forearm shoulder as one.
Achieve a decisive snap that strikes the shell cleanly
at the bowl's edge.
Empty each eggshell of its little world.

Heat the frying pan, only just enough
to melt a lump of butter the size of a nut, any nut.
Float the pan off the stove.
While the pan cools, whisk the eggs
as mildly as wind ruffles grass.
No bubbles. No froth. A slosh of cream does no harm.
Pockets of egg white will bob to the surface.
Accept this. Add salt.

When you can pat the underside of the pan
as you would pat a friend's shoulder,
return the pan to a gentle heat.
Quietly, pour in the beaten eggs. Now, leave them.
Chop some fresh tarragon, or a small tomato.
Bring this to your eggs.
Let them all get acquainted in their own time.
Drag a fork languidly through the eggs,
where a small buffer is starting to thicken.
Let your lungs fill and subside without effort. Release the breath.

Gently tour the rest of the pan.
Drag the fork around the edge again.

Now the eggs will start to yield large curds.
Observe this without urgency. Low heat. No bubbles.
Bring drifts of egg to the center,
slowly enough to feel their mute resistance
to the pull of the fork. So slight, the weight.
If curds break into pieces, you are working too hard.
You have been dragged off-center.
Stop. Get over yourself.
Let the eggs cook alone for a moment.
Honor how little they require from you.

Gather the eggs together at the center of the pan.
Coax them to turn over. Turn off the flame.
Gaze around the kitchen a moment,
take the pan from the burner.
Divide the billowy mass into portions and serve.
Eat your egg in small voluptuous bites. Do not speak.

Hard-Boiled Egg

I was born with a hard-boiled egg in my mouth. Of course I'd already peeled it, or I'd never have been passed. Stuck in the darkness of the red place, listening to muffled booms. No Mozart. Nothing to read. Sooner or later my mother would have crunched and cinched herself to regain flat abs. That would be my second chance. I was born to hit the ground running, tuck and roll, but I was slow, so slow. Like trying to learn to ride my bike, launched down a cement sidewalk. I fell as I waited for magic to strike and let me keep traveling. I was born to wait for peaches to fill out, bring the smell of summer. Like a raccoon I washed them to strip off the fuzz, I hid the pits behind the hose. I was born to wait on the ocean floor, squinting up through weight of water, looking for faint dazzle of light, afraid of distant air.

Dignitas

The taxi driver knows the way.
A moat marks the house you've come for.
Koi flirt away when you cross.
The bed is safe in a far corner.

A moat marks the house you've come for.
Pomegranate-red blanket, ice-white sheets:
the bed waits, safe in a far corner,
when you know each day too well.

Pomegranate-red blanket, ice-white sheets.
The house looks away from the city
where you know each day too well,
where the good hours are all used up.

The house looks away from the city.
Your life savings buy you nothing
when the good hours are all used up.
Pay the fare, leave a good tip.

Your life savings buy you Nothing,
the coin to float you across.
Pay the fare, leave a good tip.
The taxi driver knows the way.

Pear

You think the gods have handed you the pear,
whisper their secrets to you through the juice.
The pear's day passes with no thought of you
as darkness spreads unhurried at its core.

For everything flows, and nothing remains.
Green softens to yellow, and bite starts to yield.
Fragrance escapes and wakens your ready juices.

Proclaim what you will, the pear has its own way.
It parts from the twig and forgets the tree.
It was never in your hand, only here, where it always is.
You sigh enraptured, *It hears the gods' voices.*
Say what you like. It will not, does not hear you.

Opioid Withdrawal/Total Eclipse

Symptoms begin with restlessness	When the birds stop singing,
a general feeling of unease	when the cows are scared and dogs howl,
tingling as if the soul is	pulling at the gut, the third chakra
being rubbed with sandpaper	straining against one's own emptiness
Symptoms deteriorate	As earth regains ascendance
to a flu-like condition,	wrongness crawls over the temples,
fatal in some circumstances	when the sun sets, at noon, in the middle of the sky

carpet, n., v.

...as in bombing,
laying down death, hot and bright,
covering with orange turning
to the black that erases, smudges
like punch spilled
onto carpet, the happy host
pouring, laughing not looking,
missing the cup, a wet sticky rope
of sweet black tea and orange sherbet,
the stain that rises and rises again,
that Poe story retold, never weary,
a blow that keeps pummeling,
a blue-black stain cleaning cannot touch;
carpet woven by hands
100,000 knots of silk
tied tight, meant to last.

Ghazal of Wasted Time

Dry heat. Hail. Balmy. Cold snap chews at leaves.
Where to turn when weather confuses the leaves?

For years these two pretend they have a future.
Pursuing diverging lives, each refuses to leave.

Making small talk, she chats up his tie, gets sneers.
Who'd stay to be disdained? She chooses to leave.

Cabin under the pines, refuge for a week's writing.
She reads long pompous novels, misuses her leave.

For showy rise, each puff paste turn must be perfect.
Evenly rolled, no rips. A dull knife fuses the leaves.

The apartment is cramped, the bathroom door sticks.
No good here, though windows give views of leaves

which she collects: magenta, apricot, mottled as marble.
Keeping what is sure to fade, yet Karen muses on leaves.

Throwbacks

Hard times relieve the roses of technique,
unmingle their sources,
call out to pre-graft roots.
New canes wind and sprawl
under the open candelabra
of hybrid branches
pruned by the book.

Throwback canes sprout floribunda bouquets,
medieval canes ridiculously thick with thorns,
a flashback of petals lying flat and single,
no Fibonacci array of blades
surging clockwise, then counter,
ever increasing.

A continuity of roses,
before Homer, before history.
Petals darker than royal blood,
always the same deep red,
no matter how the plant was remade,
fed up with all that inbreeding,
revealed as *Rosewood*.
A rose is rosy as a rose.
Before there were words, there were roses.

Beautiful Leaves

So, *pot-au-feu* was just plain boiled beef.
Nothing appealed but the luscious marrow,
mashed on a chunk of baguette.
The wine was house red soft as moss.
The host timed his pours, at least four.
Laughing, you re-told our tale,
and he passed the neck of the bottle unseen
under your evoking hand.
I caught his eye   *what are you doing*
he smiled to me   *I am making him happy.*

Last to leave, we threaded around
chairs stacked up on tables.
You raised your face to the city stars,
tipped back right hard into the window box,
flattened the geraniums. I hoisted you
past the music store on rue Léopold Robert,
past the neon reflets off the boul' Raspail.
At the corner of Edgar Quinet
you sank into the friendly bench
under the streetlamp's yellow sphere
made diffuse and kind by chestnut leaves.
    Look at the leaves
        the beautiful leaves
  I've never seen   *such beautiful leaves.*

So I sat down, fine.   I looked
at those illuminated leaves,
absinthe edges outlined in lamplight.
I was tired, wanted back to our flat.
I didn't know what you knew—

   the host had poured happiness,
   the leaves were mystic love,
   time was up for the last time.
You, exalted, clear-minded, unswerving,
you knew the night should never end.

SLIP

any knot whose loop slides along the standing end.
Because these knots tighten under load,
they actually function as Nooses.

Aha: Atomic Apron

Hidden in the fold of the hem are the secrets to the atomic bomb, the equations and transitions that won the war. A white cotton apron, trimmed with satin-stitched wild roses. How can it have gone through the war and still be so pure? And the cloth, gauzy, open-weave, nothing but a net of threads. How did the secrets not leak through? Always the question no one asks out loud: *Did that really happen?* He's the one who knows. Archbishop of physicists, seventy years ago they say, he inscribed the breakthrough on the cloth, then stitched it up tight. He is now so famous that credit, blame, renown no longer concern him. All respect is temporary. He knows this, as surely as he knows everything atomic reverts, sooner or later, to hydrogen. Ad infinitum, he will remember the moment when he understood: *My God*, he'd said, *ja mei, mais non, aha.*

So Sorry

Dear Herr Doktor Profundity:

I am sorry you caught me in the check-out line reading *The National Enquirer*. If I had shown you the article about synchronicity, your irony would only have fined to a sharper pole axe. I'm sorry I stayed until 10 pm the time you invited me to lunch with your family. I tugged at my muslin bluestocking to hide the belly I didn't have, not yet. I played with your toddler daughter, made my hands into a butterfly, and she watched its slow flirt, squealed like a rabble-rouser, pounced like a caterer. You lectured her on dharma. You insisted on giving me another glimmering of wine, though I had refused; I'm sorry I kept touching your hand and giggling, though it served you right. Above all I am sorry that you convinced me to mock your wife's homicidal kim chee. It smelled all sheepdog and cheesy, must have been a good one. Strangler, you hurt her felicities in front of me. She retreated to the kitten and cried, and I ran after her to tell her I was sorry. Then you and I sat down-and-out to revoke my paper on Mephistopheles and the Nature of Evil or the Nectarine of Excess or maybe the Necktie of Evolution that you had permitted me to turn in late. In three couplets you told my thinktank had flipped: Faust was destructive, Mephistopheles the one who brought enlightenment, and consumée. *Also damnation*, I trilled, but not loudly. Mainly I was sorry that I'd worked all winter break to fireball the paper. My father drove me 40 miles to the main post office so I could find majesty before midnight. Sitting in your lizard room, scrounging for sunlight, something you would not find simple-minded, I nearly forgot my father had blacked out from a waterfall a brainstorm next morning. He would pass the first month of his last new year in the hospital. Back then, brain surgery was like stirring the brain with a fork. My Christian Scorpion grandmother crouched like a cougar, nagged God, pleaded: *You wouldn't let your choirboy David suffer, suffering is an error, a chirrup, a chimera, don't take him, I'm sorry, don't take him,* and the team of surrealists waited for her to tell them to go ahead, whatever might follow, or just to let him die right then. *He is how old?* you asked, and I told you: *Not old, just 44*, your age, like you, and you said, *I'm sorry.*

Silence and Slow Time

From the stairwell, steps dwindle, then flee.
You rub your eyes, blink at the buzzing lamps.
It seems you are in Paradise. Fall to your knees.

Low-ceilinged room with booths and desks; you glance
at empty tables, empty straight-backed chairs.
You rub your eyes, blink at the buzzing lamps.

The Glory of Sharks. The History of Hair.
The Book of Knots and Their Untying.
At empty tables, empty straight-backed chairs.

Time is art books, oversized, left lying
on armchairs dressed in herringbone, moss-green:
The Book of Knots and Their Untying.

The cooler, set for Kelvin 3 degrees,
holds water, coffee, tea and Coke in bottles.
Armchairs dressed in herringbone, moss-green,

stand in the library basement, mottled,
impersonal. The clerk says, *Wait your turn*
for water, coffee, Coke, iced tea in bottles.

Your drowsy dullness deepens with the drone.
In the stairwells, steps dwindle, then flee.
Impersonal, the clock says, *Wait your turn.*
It seems you are in Paradise. Fall to your knees.

Less Passionate Ghazal

One touch at the sagging gate and it swings open.
Clenched fists can't garden. Let your fingers open.

Never expected beginners' nor any other luck.
Drew cards so good, I let a pair of kings open.

Homeless man under grimy white plastic endures cold wind.
And you wear a chic new jacket? Let your purse-strings open.

The cat has caught a fledgling, limp with fright.
When I praise her, she mews, and its wings open.

Voice lesson: don't work so hard. Get out of your way.
Throat, breath all easy. Fearless, your voice rings open.

The lid resists your hand. Set your strength just so.
Then feel the jar, smooth as wax, unscrewing open.

Isn't always a boon to care and ask too much.
Rejoice without wanting: heart sings, "Open."

Ariel   echo of Prospero

who is satisfied to see
himself extended   his arm in flight
plucking   upending   returning
but Ariel is no more Prospero
    than candle flame
    and logs burning
are diverse elements
Ariel is no more Prospero
    than fire
    is anything but fire
    enflaming consuming
burning damp pulp down to carbon crusts

Twiggy and Me

Twiggy's legs are perfectly free of muscle.
She may be this year's phenom, sneers *Time*,
but those legs are like two white worms.
Wider than it is long, her hot pink corduroy skirt
sprouts her thighs, scarcely bigger than her ankles.
She is an English girl who drinks Cokes, not teas.

Is this what girls should look like? The question teases
at me. Her spaghetti shape is nothing like my muscles.
Twiggy's a waif with sad eyes. Her arms dangle
like Nijinski doing Petruschka, old-time.
She is the new natural. That must be why her skirts
have wide belts, to hold them up on her waist like a worm's.

Now my gym teacher laughs so hard I squirm.
When we practice, she gasps, "Ladies, ladies, don't tease!"
We are pretending to exit a VW bug, wearing mini-skirts.
Mrs. Patterson's shorts reveal eye-popping muscles
(few women strove to get buffed in those times).
and she shows us, again, how our knees have to angle.

Twiggy's hair is short as a boy's, cut at right angles.
I have Shirley Temple ringlets that twist like worms.
I scotch-tape my bangs flat, but all night isn't enough time
to tame my natural curl. Twiggy's bob frees us from teasing
our hair to Marie Antoinette-heights. Still, some of us'll
never have the good hair, nor the right legs for the skirt.

Twiggy's furry eyelashes are longer than her skirt.
I study her photo for hours, my head at an angle
absolutely guaranteed to spasm my neck muscles.
She is pale, blank as a peeled egg; nothing to be wormed

out of her. She stands for that moment in the sixties
when the revolution hit the stores. Talk about timing.

Back to homework. I'm writing a report, beating time
to *Revolution* on my sturdy calf. My history teacher is curt
about late papers, grades strict. I'm shy and ill-at-ease.
In his class, mean kids, even bullies, turn into angels.
That spring we studied all about the Diet of Worms.
Austere Luther had some serious spiritual muscle.

I'd need time to work out my angle on being a girl,
to quit skirting around like some outcast worm,
find the muscle to use my eyes and still cross all the T's.

Two-Wheeler

Sidewalks eat knees, heel of hands.
I try to land softer
but I'm no rider, no driver.
I'm diver, hostage, carried too fast.

Pull yourself together   straighten up   ride right,
find music for those two hundred muscles,
the tune everyone else dances to,
shimmering along
on two wheels' shifting tangent to the sidewalk.

Babysitter runs along behind.
She grabs the book rack
giving me another good push,
gabbling pointless advice, a crazy fever dream,

but I am elsewhere,
waiting for magic unbiddable as orgasm,
I fall and mount, fall and wait

Metaphor Blew Them Away

Undersides of mosaic wings
        sneak among clusters
        of eucalyptus nuts.

Monarchs shine like fish scales, fit close
        as artichoke petals, dangle
        light as earrings from fine wires.

Milkweed's tree-line limit good as a net
        along the 48th parallel.
        Not one wing will get past.

Gulliver took butterflies for hawks
        before he understood
scale and distance are liars.

Perspective

When Shakespeare wrote *Who steals my purse steals trash*,
it's clear he never had this purse in mind.
Fab Kate Spade purse in *Vogue* is just the kind
of A-list party I don't want to crash.

Procure this purse, your life is in the bag.
The chunk of space encompassed by yon hide
would swallow all that I might toss inside.
I'd rummage armpit deep, yet never snag.

Steel-studded leather tent! This purse will hold
a camel plus its rider. Climb on in.
Your Steinway, your Guarneri violin
would still not pay this fashion gateway's toll.

Persephone, who gave up more for worse,
says, *Honey, let it go*: *it's just a purse.*

Endless Water

You dive off a high white cube, no railings, no board, into the deep ocean fifty feet below. The waves are pale blue, ruffled and regular as piped icing on a vast cake. Swim, crawl, paddle like a dog over to the white raft, that loose tooth in the ocean's wide mouth, haul out and pivot and launch yourself to swim back. Climb up the flush ladder, the cold iron rungs, back up to the deck. The clock is running. *Fast as you can*, your teammates are panting, the next one is waiting, one after the other until someone gives out. Always alone in the ocean. Try to convince yourself: you only have to swim through the top part. Never mind the endless water underneath. This is not the Olympics. You are soldiers and this stands for war. Winning saves everyone waiting at home. The other team loses its crops and songs and country. No silver medals. The other is consumed in tribute. Its people must labor to fill their mouths with the enemy's words. If you stop to eat lunch—panic at the plunge—scramble as you hang onto the raft, your legs clawing through the water, instead of pulling out with a clean vault—if your cold hands scrabble at the round metal rungs—defeat will be your fault. Better to be swallowed up.

Disco Jukebox Sestina Blues

Back when I believed in dance, in razzmatazz,
to dance was to live! and living was zigzagging
to the synchronicities of the jukebox,
boogying with the door of the refrigerator
for partner, dodging the macraméd fern pot, cuspidor
for journals of record and old exam books (blue).

Some mornings, I danced through my ablu-
tions, dreaming a world of razzmatazz,
hit all my marks on the beat. Others, I'd cuss bad, or
weep a bit, do my stretches, zigzagging
from desk to floor to refrigerator,
looking for *wattitiz wattitiz* on the jukebox.

It sounds corny as country on the jukebox,
but I did think love could come out of the blue
and make my life dance, like that ad: *refrigerator
meets the right cleanser, and—razzmatazz!
a disco ball of sparks zigzagging.*
The party where I met him had no cuspidor.

In bed he brought me only to the cusp. *J'adore*,
I moaned, looking for the funk of the jukebox's
single falling into place, not all this zigzagging
and fooling around just short of *l'heure bleue*.
He play-growled, "Next time, baby, I'll razz your tazz,"
and I giggled like the bowl rattling on the refrigerator.

He was sweet, but dumb like a refrigerator.
Thought Cupid was derived from cuspidor.
Anyhow, my one night of razzmatazz
was a dumb idea too. Later, I chewed kabobs

at the Greek place. Damn, I was blue,
as I watched the off-kilter gyros zigzagging.

No, I was getting no buzz from zigzagging.
Time to use the Force and clean out the refrigerator,
get some new tunes for that horn I blew
(liberated? sometimes I felt more like a cuspidor),
some songs you might not find on the jukebox,
to hold out for the right berries, those razz of Tasmania.

Like a zigzagging drunk who's clocked himself on the cuspidor,
time for me to chill out. Plug in the refrigerator, toss the jukebox.
All that razzmatazz was just giving me the blues.

Oak Apples

Glossy leather skin
shriveling to a dry planetoid
smaller than an egg, falling back
on its armature. Cracks betray
craters, pinholes, the debut
of forty-one departing gall wasps.
The oak swelled this squat gray sphere
to wall off artless seepage,
wanting a prison, making a nursery.

The Blues

I rushed, I stopped to discover
postcard Mediterranean
and glacier blue
are the same blue, twice contained.

Glaciers loom ancient yet recent
as Lascaux bison stampeding on stone,
ice ages still piling and ebbing,
fled futures our bodies still remember.

This year, two miles into mountains,
nothing but the drift of sun-dried scree.
Twenty years back, I'd stopped
and stepped over the shoulder
right onto a glacier's latest snow,

holding that blue made of air
emptied out of cities, lakes, lungs.
Outside turned inward,
most private blue on earth.

I'd filled my hand with water,
a gift. I lifted, I sipped.
Blue so pure it lit me up
as though I'd gulped a star.

GRANNY

also known as Thief Knot, Grief Knot.
Can release suddenly and unpredictably.

Acknowledgement, In Other Words

Clara her name, *clear light*,
my mother's mother, cast down and out.
Encased in the one black sateen dress,
she was seamstress on-call to ladies, nothing special.
Perhaps her hoarse voice held her back,
or her stutter that could not be tamed.
I never noticed, only her voice coming gentle
when she grabbed and waggled my cheek:
You're gorgeous! (always news to me).

I invaded closets in her duplex,
sniffed raspberry syrup in the bottle,
unfurled rolled recycled ribbons, built walls
from the thousand paper cups,
but one game was hers alone.
She liked to glean words, untangle
& sort anagrams, her own secret good time.
I peeked while her unschooled mind
decanted from *acknowledgement*:
gnawed—neglect—welcome—melon—gleam.

When she was my age now, an aneurysm
breached her backed-up brain,
swept her words from their shelves,
leaked deep red through the weakened wall
that no needle could sew shut.
Elegant—knot—owlet—lament.

Papa

There is no such thing as a baby, only a baby and a caretaker.
—D. W. Winnicott, British child psychoanalyst

He knows the ways of giant pumpkins. We're talking three-quarters of a ton, pumpkins to make pick-up trucks groan, drag low, gouge ruts into asphalt. Tight next to the heirloom chickens, many are fruited but one is chosen, one single pumpkin fed by ninety square yards of vine. He stoked the soil five years to fuel leaves tall and broad as lotus, waist-high stalks thick as eggs, you should see the stem of the queen, thick as my big-boned wrist. She lies at anchor, a diving bell, an emerging island. *That's my baby girl,* he says, *only one month old.* July. August, September, October, drinking long stretches of light and heat. How fast her shadow lengthens. Score the pretenders with your nail before you twist them off, watch the spilling growth pop them apart like a dropped dictionary falling open to *horticulture.*

Bel Canto for the King

Velvet Elvis in white Stretch-velour,
in a stupor, a torpor of Demerol.
No time for languor in the Vegas lounge.
The colonel harangues,
Who brung you that barbital,
you cur, you dog, you hound?
Flaccid Elvis languishes,
an oblivious meringue.
Yet not eight thousand impersonations
can deflate nor abate Elvis.
Elvis ate sandwiches
of bacon, bananas, nutty butter.
Demerol and methadone
and loneliness ate Elvis.

History, with Rugelach

I heel-and-toe along the sidewalk squares.
No one holds my hand to keep me close.
No women are allowed past temple doors.

It seems I'm on my own. I'm maybe four.
Men rush up to the passage. In they go.
I can't work out why someone wants me here.

Flat squared-off grass. I still don't know who's who.
I stand, my fence-post legs locked straight and braced.
A hedge of black wool coats blocks off my view.

Dark hats pulled low and close don't cover mouths
or eyes squeezed shut or what the faces keen.
Another language wadded in those mouths,
another country under powdered skin.

A stranger's house. I hope for rugelach,
find only pumpernickel, dry, two-toned,
playing at marbled pound cake. Stupid trick.

No sweetness, no redemptive chocolate,
no cinnamon to warm my silent tongue,
no walnuts, no tart chew of apricot.

I'm pressed to prickly faces, squirm and cringe.
Like sugar, she's so sweet. They swoop and kiss,
and I must let them. Who explains such things?

My Mother the Illusionist

Watch her make disappear
a pound of lox
with her bare hands,
shred after shred
from the plate I'd spread.
Hear her conjure
Nothing for me.

Smoky fishy balm lingers,
softens her fingertips,
loosens her misdirecting tongue.

All true magicians understand
the power of emptiness,
its triumph over taint.
In a trance she conceals
the bagel, the cream cheese.

She banishes sweet satiety
at least a week at a time,
every bite insisting
the count must start all over again.

Her signature illusion:
a bite can be undone.
Takes endless distraction
to erase the teeth marks of her passage.

Fluted papers peeled
from cornbread muffins
stack up at her plate until
she palms them into her purse.
Did you see that?

Bob Hope at the River Glen Psych Unit

He stands in the middle where the halls all meet, ready to cast his fame, a fly tied by an expert. Aides flow around and past his boulder to hear last shift's report. Visiting relatives look down at the hard dark carpet, bracing against double-edged greetings. It's no USO gig. Bob sports a crisp summer suit, tan as canned gravy, a white shirt yellowed by the lights. Two years since he's seen his niece, and she's in no hurry to skip lunch, walk away from her fried shrimp to see him. His big-time eyes dart glances, ready to break into that big-star smile, throw a gracious word, a calculated quip to snag a big-mouth fan. Already his heart is half-way out the door to the Caddy and the bucket seats, the AC, the laugh track.

Jitterbug

You have to understand:
he should have died
when fever torched his otic nerve,
scalded his inner ear.
Grandma bargained, connived, even
changed his name to change God's mind:
David, always outmatched,
yet understanding the swing of sling.
The odds shorted him, every time.

Somehow he knew music,
sold vinyl in Hollywood after school.
His heart beat 4/4 like the blues,
just right for a jitterbug slow enough for flair,
to place, to plant the back foot
so the wave snaps right up your spine
to your thrown-back head.
Loved the cool grunt of the bass
sounding diminished thirds,
augmented sevenths. Vibes poured
through the pencil
he held like a straw between his teeth,
eraser braced on the turntable base.

The man could dance.
Taught me the off-kilter tilt of hips
kept balanced by the partner's hand,
shoulders spiraled around the core,
each of us styling, saved from falling
by the back-beat back-step.

He'd raise his arm and I'd strut under,
turning as natural as walking.
We'd move into the snazzy draw,
hands sliding along the other's arms,
no words needed for the trick
of snagging fingertips,
catching and pulling back to the center,
leaning and returning,
solid on the beat he could not hear.

The Art of Coin Fishing

The pockets of his blazer sag with books.
Ronsard's *Amours*. Cervantes. La Fontaine.
His thread-the-needle scarf, his cigarette
somehow suspended at his lip, unlit,
mark him as Latin Quarter retiree.
He's still a man of letters, philosophe.

He fishes from the fountain, casts a glance
at me between his casts, he reels
his line, inspects his catch, suppresses his smile.
In this Paris pocket park, I'm hooked.

The fountain yields to him
Euros, francs and kronen, Dutch and Danish,
Queen Margarethe in bright profile.
The pool's distorting waters
bring coins' faces near the surface.

You can profit from this sport, madame.
The line, wound round his hand,
drags a little dust pan that
stirs up tourists' wishes.
The pennies? only minnows.
Best catch them and release, madame.
Be patient and they'll grow up into Euros.
Really, madame, no one cares for pennies.

Our Lady of the Red Potatoes

Our Lady of the Red Potatoes
has set her altar on a city bench.
She hunches small. No star-blue mantle
shielding her from winter light.
Hunger-thin and gray, not old,
in Rhino Records' parking lot she calls
Red potatoes, red, six for a dollar.

Her eyes squeeze shut. I watch
her roughened hands
read each potato's face.
She listens for their low voices.
Her hands receive the messages
her gods have scrawled there.
Behold, she hands to me
six red potatoes, red, six for a dollar,
thin-skinned potatoes bigger than my fist.

I rasp potato peel, twirl out their eyes,
prepare to receive the mystic meal
of red potatoes, red, six for a dollar.
No healing or redemption from our lady,
just nature's artless poison, pure green gift
of alkaloids, red potatoes green as glass.
They are fallen from the earth into the light,
sun-stroked like their lady.

To Die in Cochabamba (I Will Not Die in Paris)

Cochabamba, green valley at the mountaintop,
umbilical scar high on the equator.
No one dies in Cochabamba.
I will die in Cochabamba.

Cochabamba of eternal spring,
no longest night, no shortest day.
Streams freeze hard after sundown,
winter comes every night in Cochabamba.

Cochabamba of bum leg, the *fútbol* ploy.
The center herds the ball past rival feet,
threads it down the field on bamboo legs.
Fans shout eternal spring in Cochabamba.

Cochabamba, hit samba of *Carneval*.
Close the window, that cochabamba
is getting on my last nerve, I tell the nurse,
but she is busy slipping morphine under my tongue.
She cups my face in her dry hand,
and my eyes, lips, bum leg relax, *Ay, mi cochabamba.*

It seems in Cochabamba everyone knows,
but I don't understand, I never have.
I am a plane crash in Cochabamba,
aisle lights down the center in the dark.

Fairest

We dallied all day at the Renaissance Faire.
Lace-up bodice of my milkmaid costume
bared my indoor shoulders to sunburn.
I'd already had warning from the sooth-
sayer: *Don't show too much or you'll be sore.*
You thought she gave everyone that line.

I braved the fencing booth, flirted my line
at the blushing blond staffer, Harold the Fair:
Prithee, noble sir, let me handle your sword.
Sun-dazed kids slumped on hay bales, unaccustomed
to loud hours spent yelling *Varlet, forsooth!*
slashing and thwacking each other. Bobbie Burns

and kindred Scots snaked across drought-tanned burns
in their anachronistic bagpipe-conga lines.
SoCal Renaissance kitsch. Our kisses soothed
and quickened. We were in love, and all was fair.
Photographer caught you doing up my costume,
kissing my cleavage under oaks. Hawks soared.

On the lookout for my girlfriend. She was sore,
enraged you'd left a wife for me. So burned-up
you wanted marriage. And she'd lent me the costume!
Her guy said if she pushed he'd leave; she toed the line.
I'd known her through 10 years, 20 men. So unfair,
her sudden rules of honor. How she seethed.

Shakespeare would have understood. The Bard saith,
brain-bound Hamlet was *punished with distraction sore.*
Fool, he could have been wooing Ophelia the fair.
You and I had tried to part, met only heart-burn.

Now, on a borrowed lute, you plucked the melodic line,
your knowing hand adding flourish, a lacy costume.

You'd worshiped music all your life, accustomed
to making your own small joy, while you soothed
the next rescue who'd thrown you her lifeline.
We were no sin, we needed no confessor.
Every astounded touch did, would always burnish.
All our photos were soft-focus. A day full and fair.

Later, burn-up on re-entry, traffic a mile-long line
of costumed players. Nobles, jesters, maidens fair,
drowsy and soothed by turkey legs big as dinosaurs'.

Monsieur Saluki

He's installed in front of the cemetery
and we pass him, on our way to the Métro station,
on our way to the café with the guide dog.
He argues with himself in reasoned discourse,
laying out his points, weighing each in his hands,
one against the other. He nods: *well said*.
Full hair springing silver frames brown eyes
dark and liquid as a Saluki. Monsieur Saluki.
He surveys us holding hands, settles
his fringed red scarf like Lautrec's Aristide;
he snags my eye and calls to me: *Mais souriez, ma belle!*
A beat until my French clicks: *Come on, sweetheart, smile!*
and when I hear, I smile to him as sweet as ever I can.
He tips his face up to the leafing white alders,
he sighs, *Oh, to be in love in springtime.*

Stop and try our Homemade Pie

We pause on the long stretch
from Kelso to Sutherlin.
They serve the solid crust
unbuttered underbaked unloved,
pale and dense as particle board.

Overhear the old man at the next table,
deflated version of his pastor
who promises *everything you ever wanted
over on that other side*
who is leaning in close,
trying to out-talk death.

Will I get back my teeth?
How old will I be?

        Can't tell a lie with custard pie.
        I order custard, and that's why.
        This slice of pie's a lying cheat,
        not worth the time to cook nor eat.

We ate blueberries all the way down to California,
we crammed them by the handful into our mouths,
each dark burst staining, perfuming our fingers.

Real Poem

Open mike, she comes up to ask me, were those real poems, or did I just make them up. I confess: *I just make them up.* Her look says *I thought as much.* So many years I have faked it, getting credit for stuff I just made up. What you are reading here, for instance. It's not a real poem, just one I made up. This poem did not come from a certified breeder, someone who could vouch for the pedigree of the parents. Nah, it's a mutt, a Heinz 57, a tabby-tortie-tiger cat, maybe even missing a tail. At the computer it will not leave me alone. *Make a real poem out of me,* it hisses, stalking across the keyboard, *make me a real poem.* At my desk, I made a nest for it from my grandmother's shawl, the one she crocheted even before she married my grandfather the head baker of Łodz. The poem deliberately lies sprawled across the paper I'm trying to write on, or it swarms up my shoulder, then lodges under my chin. I can't even see what my hand is doing. Sometimes I try to write without looking, but my hands crawl a row up or a key over, and the whole thing transposes into code, spilling out and leaking onto the table, disappearing into the carpet. Sometimes I lose track of the lines and go right off the rails, maybe even over the edge. But, when the poem is satisfied I am not ignoring it, it lets me write. It curls up in the shawl-nest and sleeps, breathing in quick little bursts, snoring tiny snores, feet twitching as it dreams.

Older woman

Lacquered dandelion in full puff,
one breath away from gone,
the gauzy veil of careful hair floats at anchor
over her freckled eggshell skull.
She has become the opposite of shrewd.
The memory of habit
finds her, assiduous,
coaxing the relic of her crown
into its old place.

The Babinski

Monitors grind, and light from nowhere
comes soft as the sole of my aunt's foot
somehow cleared of spur and callus

My cousin strokes her mother's hand, calls her name,
the blurred Rs of childhood returning
as she tries to override the bled-out brain

The nurse hisses *don't agitate the patient,* chivvies us out,
but my clinical thumbnail has already creased her sole
and got no answer. First-year, assessment of reflex:
if the toes don't splay, well…

Estate Sale

An ecru beaded top, and champagne furs,
the score of Lakmé with the Bell Song marked,
twelve coral linen napkins: these were hers.
The neighbors come to peep. Cars throng to park.

I see her sporting silver pixie hair.
The kitchen's apple-papered, open plan,
and yellow Caution tape marks every stair,
each jarring drop from where your steps began.

I think it was her husband who went first.
No books of his except the PDR,
2003. Been years since he was versed
in pulmonology and beating par.

There is no moral here to apprehend.
Someone cleans up. The world is without end.

GORDIAN

Alexander the Great attempted to untie the sacred knot but could not find an end to make a start. He then sliced it in half with a stroke of his sword, producing the required ends, annihilating the knot. That night there was a violent thunderstorm. Alexander's prophet Aristander called it a sign that Zeus was pleased.

Double Abecedarian at Forest Lawn

Aneurysm took Aunt Thelma, whose coma raised such buzz.
Bleeding in the brain gave her six months of dying slowly.

Caused your mother's death too, Mom, at just fifty-six.
Didn't I sob when Thelma died, harder because I knew
ending when I heard it. I prayed: Blessed St. Nureyev,
find me the footing to pick through family kudzu.

Guaranteed: now there is no one left to get my point.
Here's a cold hug at the coffin. My mother's body stiffens.

I am held off while Thelma's husband, philanderer,
jerk, weeps hard. For this I will need more than IQ.
Knot in my throat knows you expect me to beg to make up,
like I've always done—yet this time, I cannot go
make my grief small, not on Forest's zombie-green lawn.

Now something inside me has had its day, goes dim.
Outdoors, L.A. noon, white glare hits our black memorial.

Plaques surround us where your glare is a basilisk
quivering with tears, ready for me to plead. Aunt AJ
runs home to set out bagels, but you wait, irrational as pi,
still wronged, and angry at me, as usual? Well, yeah.
Traditional black suit is perfect for waiting, harping, accusing.

Unplanned words sprout in my mouth, open to me leaf by leaf.
Variations on if-not-now, when? launch, and now I'm free.

Want to know, really, why you won't be the one I've missed?
X-acto knives, your words were meant to cut me down in public.

Yes, I was glad to be rid of my long impossible job.
Zilch to want back, except for Aunt Thelma.

Conductor

> Suicide by train is popular in many developed countries.
> Without ready access to firearms, suicidal people often turn to trains . . .
> —Der Spiegel, July 27 2011

Once it happens
you can't remember before:
innocent, barreling into the tunnel,
shooting out at each station
like a dolphin from a dim green pool.
Pneumatic doors inhale open, puff shut,
lock with a solid thump.

Up and down the line, fifty times a day,
it's a long slow song. You
feel the rumble as much as hear it.
In your dim green trance
the muffled words retain wonder:
Vorsicht, Türe werden geschloßen.
Careful, the doors are closing.

The first time someone decides
only darkness will answer,
he hides out in the tunnel
before he steps out in front of the train
as if he knows where he's going.
He steps out at you, dying at you,
daring you to stop in time.

Now when the doors close
they seal you in. You are the human bullet
shot into the tunnels, hoping no one
will block the light up ahead,
each station one minute's reprieve.

Burrowing Song

A song burrowed into a woman's head. It got in when someone said, "Oh, that's just dandy." *C&H, C&H, Mommy uses it to bake her cakes. She makes the greatest cookies cakes and candy— they're dan-dan-dandy!* When the woman was in her bed, she could hear it upstairs.

C&H, C&H, Mommy uses it to bake her cakes. The woman called a pest control service, the one with the man dressed like an undertaker and carrying the big heavy mallet. She asked them to kill the song. *It needs to be fed*, they said, *don't you have some cookies, cakes or candy?* "Oh, that's just dandy," the woman told them, and then she wept. Her blood pressure went up, so her GP prescribed meds. The song still played, only now in a chromatic scale, like Bach gone inbred.

Finally, the woman packed up her red Keds and left the house. The song had become part of the plumbing and stayed behind. Cool, she thought, at last I've got the damned thing balked. *Who is the coolest guy who is what am? Fast-talking slow-walking good-looking Mohair Sam.*

Now she has a safe tune and always carries it with her. When she sings it silently, the tune can always drive away a burrowing song.

Komisch

Kafka is funny but no one laughs. I will explain, then you too will not laugh. Kafka is funny because he writes in German. All those weighty words strung together: German is a pratfall waiting to happen. Kafka knows he is funnier than Proust, who clowns, strumming and fingering a tennis racket like a banjo while enjoying a vacation with his parents. Kafka would not descend to such stunts. Also, his parents never take vacations.

What is funny? Insist on a corner as the way out. Try a door made only to block your way, only to be shut in your face—pure slapstick. Joyce can't be funny unless he is lewd, but Kafka won't work blue. A kidney in the pocket, the wind blowing words away: such cheap effects. Singing mice, girls with webbed hands, writing a punishing line ten thousand times—the Marx Brothers would kill for bits like that, and Chaplin would die to get hold.

How, how to learn to be funny. Start as a vegetarian with a butcher for a father. What could be more absurd? Perhaps, money to make up for losing your hand? Perhaps, getting less money for losing half your hand. Then figure how much savaged hand is enough to matter. A thumb, yes, but what about a pinkie? At the Workers' Compensation office, Kafka ponders such things every day, all day long, and then they give him money. What does it mean? Ask a jackdaw who's just crossed the road.

Passing Through

People feel good at the Bible Belt Café. The passing woman hears three women meditating over a laptop, exegesis in the air. They are puzzling over the Old Testament, wondering out loud how someone could be Jewish. They have never met anyone Jewish. What could it mean, to be Jewish? Though she is merely passing, she helps out: *It means we don't believe the Messiah has come.*

The passing woman threads her way through the Bible Belt Café and hears no trace of doubt. Again she discovers herself a spy passing easily among the others. She knows the carols on the radio, all the words, though these are not her songs, though she goes silent on every *Christ*. Holiday coffees hold cold-weather flavors in balmy SoCal. Gingerbread, pumpkin pie spice, eggnog, candy cane mocha. *Those aren't religious, they're seasonal,* says her friend. *They are for the North, for snow, and Nick is a saint,* she thinks. Wherever she goes, four-pointed stars, and long lines to sit in Santa's lap. *Didn't you ever sit in Santa's lap?* Yes, but he was only a man.

The passing woman hears two pastors talk about their deacons, their youth groups. One gives thanks: *Football brought me closer to Jesus.* The thermal sleeve on her cardboard cup offers eternal refills of worldly coffee in the name of the Samaritan woman and the outsider at the well. Your choice of French or Vienna roast, even espresso bitter as original sin.

The passing woman lowers her voice when she says *Jewish*. Eyes cast down, she edges past the busy tables. Latte plus a good tip rents a table for three hours. The passing woman draws from her own well. She bypasses Holy Writ to spin her own thread, fragile as corn silk. God has spoken to her but she knows she is no prophet. He has used deeds not words. Once He twisted her tongue to keep her secrets. Once He stabbed her stomach, doubled her over, to tell her to stand up and run. Once He smote her flat to show her that leaven was gone from her life. He doesn't hand out damnation for prayers or praise. He speaks only with thunder, and bolts of lightning.

Macht Frei

The girl who walked with gravel in her shoes used to be a German girl, before she looked for pain for the sake of her Papa, such an ardent SS officer. He named her Sigrid, *beautiful victory*. Her raw feet told her
   entfliehen durch fliegen allein   *you can escape only if you fly.*
Her mother never asked about the stains, kept silence for them both.

She took the flying leap long after, far away. Her human weight was too much pressure on her soles. Her voice, her accent, her out-of-order words were gravel in her ears, until she headed for the ground to take the load off. Her suicide note breathed out so many thoughts: how silence whispered just out of hearing, how shouting shrugged off words; how no shoe fit right enough for her to wear; how her mother always mended her socks, how her father had loved stained glass. In Berlin at the end of the Final Solution, shock waves slammed, popped church windows from their sockets, and the air filled with brightness. One thousand flying shards of Gothic glass found him, sure as needles.

Oneiric CV

I can do anything until October 9, 2014, when I will die.

I have found myself naked in front of people for more than fifty years. I have brazened it out. I have looked for clothing and struggled to dress without drawing more attention to myself. Only last night I said, *Damn, naked again?*

I have secrets. I have kept them and I have told them, as required. I can prepare ritual matzoh to induce mystical experiences. With no training except watching TV I have defended myself in courts. I have escaped wolves by rhythmically waving striped socks.

I admit: I can fly up into the air but I cannot stay aloft. The train station will not let me find it. I cannot steer a car from the back seat. At an orgy, all I did was watch and brood. *Sure, it looks like fun, but—is it Art?*

I have fed cats, from kittens to toms big as panthers. I have been rescued by a dying horse. Even my goldfish have faked their own deaths. I have communicated by radio xylophone. I met my distant cousins, the ones who asked *why did the chicken cross the road.* They gave me the answer.

I have returned to college and high school more times than I can count. I have never missed a class or been unprepared for a test; I just don't know when to give up.

Please, check my references. Bill Clinton and Carl Jung are waiting to hear from you. Don't contact my mother or Bob Dylan, not until they get over the times I tried to kill them. The last time I saw my father was at a party. He was wearing his lucky yellow shirt. We never got to talk, but he smiled and he waved. He had read my lips.

Northern Lights

In Alaska there is no fruit from trees, light long enough only to grow berries as Northern Lights flicker, tickling raspberries and blackberries like grow-lights twitching weed into leafy green. Here berries grow the light day long until day shrinks and night reaches in, minutes dropping away like water dripping off roofs, never fast enough not to freeze, slow enough to extend ice until light is stored in stalactites, but never in fruit, time too short to develop seeds or hope, nothing but rhubarb, astringent beyond sugar's power to sweeten, beyond the reach of a world where bees survive winter.

Planet Janet

When something flips in Planet Janet's molten core, her magnetic field reverses. Suddenly North becomes South, positive becomes negative. Good luck keeping your feet on the ground. And winds break records for force, die down, leave tidal drifts of sand, exploded trees. *Who did this,* grouses Planet Janet. And continents arise from the oceans, break up and sail apart, hooking up with other continents. Fossil records don't match creation myths, but fossils are stuck in the catastrophe that turned them fossil in the first place. And what's with those active volcanos?

Planet Janet isn't a young planet any more, but she acts like one. Planet Janet likes to call at 2 a.m., drunk, sentimental. *We were on fire,* she says with a quaver, *I think about you all the time.* Planet Janet has more crust than any other planet. No hard-working granite. After the rains, rivers flow in new-carved beds. Water seeps right through porous lava foam. Planet Janet thinks her native flora are found nowhere else, but she's got it all turned around. Introduced crops just never flourish. Settlers may struggle to survive, but they never will take hold.

My Uncle the Perfectionist

Salt falls, veiling his plate. He's talking about some movie, but when he shakes that maraca, no one hears anything else, no one can look away from the shimmer of grains. You want to clatter over his sound track, you want to ask him *Don't you taste it yet? How would you call it, taste-deaf? tongue-blind?* He's got the Cro-Magnon avalanche, that infamous cliff of a forehead, but he acts like there's no frontal lobe to fill it. No self-checking, never mending, never ever amending. He'll try anything a time or six, burnt child eying the fire. Everyone else sees the whipped cream pie flying, yet another slapstick gag become shtick. His new girlfriend is getting her 7-day chip at AA for the eighth time. When he dug a hole to set a trap, he fell in. He never notices the foreshock that has everyone else ducking for cover. He should know by now, but to him everything always tastes the same. Soon he'll drip tears, contrite all over again, the same damned crime, the same tell-tale flavor. What has been will be.

Ghazal before Memory

A song we'd danced to jarred my memory.
Our first clumsy kiss is starred in memory.

Heloïse, banished to a nunnery, did not repent.
She lived but to write of Abelard, the memory.

Hemingway lived here, where Verlaine died.
In Paris I used the camera's card for memory.

Our linguist friend in France, abruptly dead.
We ate pistou then drank Ricard in memory.

I learned: while learning, all roads climb uphill.
Hands, knees are healed but scarred in memory.

I paced iambic, chanting *No longer mourn for me...*
Forty years on, and still I hold the Bard in memory.

When his time comes, she will howl and clutch.
How could Karen grieve less hard in memory?

"Still Life with Anemones," "Room at Arles"

Now tendrils writhe up from the canvas, spill
across the yellow frame in arsenic green,
his telltale color for what wants to fill

and crowd him out until there's only vines
to halt his brush, then overrun his face.
Too late, now, for the vase's heavy line.

Bed washstand chair: the doctor's house at Arles.
There is no way to walk across the room.
Each shabby piece has warped this smallest world.

His eye advises him not to assume,
not to rely on any point of sight.
The chair, the bed, the window do not dream

the same great yellow field to hold them all,
and where they don't agree, the air bleeds out.
He cannot step across. The floorboards fail

to guide him where he never can arrive.
There is no place to be, no way to leave.

Dayenu: Genug

Forgive me, Bubbe.
I couldn't learn French fast enough.
When the department kicked me out
I marched over and majored in German.
Took my junior year in Munich,
learned how Germans play tennis,
how they make their beds
without top sheets.

Forgive me, Bubbe.
They spoke my language in Germany,
everything that spoke to me,
Truth through Art, *Dichtung und Wahrheit*,
Apollo on plundered Greek vases.
I looked up every new word, Bubbe.
I slept heavy, twelve hours a night,
working so hard to learn German.
Even in my dreams I tried to speak German.
Even in my dreams I couldn't find the words.

I saw *Cabaret* dubbed into German,
heard them say *Tomorrow Belongs to Me.*
I ate Sacher torte   wienerschnitzel   blood oranges.
I ate sausages of pork from Nuremberg.

My roommate was a dental student.
From soap she carved models, teeth big as my head.
We picnicked in the German Black Forest,
picked wild raspberries, *Himbeeren*, heavenly berries
so ready we tickled them into our hands,
ate them up right there.

In December I hitchhiked to Salzburg
to hear Mozart in his cold white church.
I lined up in Berlin
to hear St. Matthew's Passion
and *Tristan und Isolde,* so many hours,
transported, Bubbe, by Jesus and opera.

Somehow I learned the German rules.
God help me, Bubbe,
I even passed for German.
That should have been enough.

My German was inspired, *begeistert.*
I was there to learn to speak like a native,
and like a native did I speak, even
with a charming little Bavarian accent,
just enough to sound suppressed,
and German.

German guys saw me dancing, put up
with my vocabulary from Goethe.
Their fathers had all been stationed at the Russian front.
Like you, Bubbe, they found me pretty.
She is judged! She is saved!
Oh stay a while, thou art so fair.

Winter Solstice, he kissed me.
You would have seen it coming, Bubbe,
wouldn't you? Forgive me.
We both spoke German.
There is only so much I can tell you, Bubbe.

A doctor smiled, prescribed me the Pill.
No one else had asked if I was Jewish.

Munich: what a place to try to call home.
Not even thirty years after Shoah,
I hoped chamber music and courtly love,
chewy sour bread, perfect accent,
would enliven me, enlighten me, change me,
supply my missing piece, bleach out my central stain,
which was nothing to do with being Jewish,
and everything to do with my mother's tongue.

In May, I swam in a lake fed by glacier melt,
clean and chilled, so cold
my ears roared *get out, get out. Heraus, heraus.*
I turned dizzy, I nearly went under, I almost drowned
in four scant feet of green water.

But Bubbe! if you could have seen
those forest clearings from the Brothers Grimm,
those spot-lit tenors and altos,
those cathedrals, Bubbe,
houses of light and shadow,
city grime outside, but within, a ceiling
of midnight blue and golden stars
so perfected, so unattainable, so Deutsch—
you'd forgive me, Bubbe.

Knots and Their Untying

See how easy others write of knots.
Books show pliant ropes
lying over and under. Loaded knots
cannot be undone by crushing.
Always the challenge, pulling against holding.
For mathematicians there are no knots, only
the counting of loops and crossings.
All knots are Gordian, made to slice.
Knot knuckle netting knitting:
not one related to another.
Sounds entwined
yet nothing ties the words together.

I learned knots that would not hold
in the enduring mystery
of tying my shoes.
Others found it easy, quick.
My unclever fingers worked
to manage the weaving.
Hold pinched what you cannot see.
Pull tight, not too soon, not too slow.

Untying a knot, easy
as talking to people who do not listen.
Persuade the fold to release both parts,
though the center promises to hold forever
against tugging and anger, hunger and haste.
Each knot works to be one though it is two,
two moving back to back,
mirrored without looking,
craning to catch the other pretending to oneness.

Tie a knot for memory, to outwit
the gap between you and your desire
when it eludes you, reminds you
      it is not you   it is not yours
You are not the string around your finger,
holding close what wants to flee.
Step out of your shoes, unbind your feet.
Time to walk away.

About the Author

Karen Greenbaum-Maya is a retired clinical psychologist, former German major, occasional photographer, and two-time Pushcart nominee. She earned her B.A. from Reed College in 1973 (German Language and Literature) and her Ph.D. from the California School of Professional Psychology in 1982 (Clinical Psychology). Besides her professional activities, she reviewed restaurants for the Claremont Courier for five years, sometimes in heroic couplets, sometimes imitating Hemingway. She has managed a congressional campaign, has sung in a local opera company, and has developed cookie recipes for commercial use. She returned to poetry in 2008, and her work appears frequently in journals and anthologies. She co-hosts Fourth Sundays, a monthly poetry series in Claremont, California, and "Garden of Verses," an annual day-long reading of nature poems in Claremont's Rancho Santa Ana Botanical Garden. Kattywompus Press publishes her two chapbooks, *Burrowing Song* (2013) and *Eggs Satori* (2014).